Strode's Coll

Sophocles

AUTHORED by Eddie Borey
UPDATED AND REVISED by Jordan Berkow

COVER DESIGN by Table XI Partners LLC
COVER PHOTO by Olivia Verma and © 2005 GradeSaver, LLC

BOOK DESIGN by Table XI Partners LLC

Published by GradeSaver LLC, www.gradesaver.com

First published in the United States of America by GradeSaver LLC. 2000

GRADESAVER, the GradeSaver logo and the phrase "Getting you the grade since 1999" are registered trademarks of GradeSaver, LLC

ISBN 978-1-60259-109-7

Printed in the United States of America

For other products and additional information please visit
http://www.gradesaver.com

Table of Contents

Table of Contents

Biography of Sophocles (496 BC-406 BC)

The Greek playwright Sophocles was born in 496 BC at Colonus, near Athens. Unlike his younger contemporary, the often-misunderstood Euripides, Sophocles had the fortune of being revered for his genius during his own lifetime. He lived to the age of ninety, and his life coincided with the great golden age of the city-state of Athens. Sophocles came from a stable, well-to-do family, and from the beginning it seemed that he was blessed in every way. Handsome, wealthy, and well-educated, Sophocles lived and died as one of Athens' most beloved citizens.

In 468 BC, his debut dramatic production took first prize at the festival of Dionysis - no small feat for a beginner in his twenties, especially considering that among his competitors was the great Aeschylus. By 450 BC, Sophocles had written some two dozen plays. He was the most prolific of the three great Greek tragedians, writing 120 plays over the span of his remarkable career. Only seven complete plays survive. He received the prize at the Dionysia a total of 24 times - more than Aeschylus or Euripides - and in the years that he competed and did not win, he took second place. Since playwrights produced trilogies for the Dionysia, this impressive record means that 72 of Sophocles' plays were first-place winners.

Sophocles' most famous plays are the Theban plays, also known as *The Oedipus Cycle*. *The Oedipus Cycle* includes *Oedipus Rex*, *Oedipus at Colonus*, and *Antigone*. Though they're often performed as a trilogy, Sophocles did not write these plays, and they were not performed in sequence - despite the related plots. The Cycle documents the doomed lineage of Oedipus the King, who killed his father, married his mother, and discovered both crimes after the fact, leading his descendants to suffer from a curse upon his family.

Sophocles was an innovator in his art: he improved stage scenery, reduced the importance of the chorus, and, most significantly, added a third speaking actor to the traditional two. He made some of the best use of this last convention, writing scenes that capitalized on the dramatic potential of three on-stage actors. Of the three tragedians, he has what is arguably the best sense of drama and pacing. His plays are cleanly made, tightly constructed, and filled with beautiful poetry. In many ways, he was a conservative man, and was a firm believer in Athenian religion and Athenian government. Sophocles' characters are tragically flawed, but their heroic stature is beyond question. The larger-than-life attributes that make them great are the same traits that cause their destruction, but their greatness is preserved, even emphasized, by Sophocles' unique dramatic sensibility. They are far from the complex and troubling psychological portraits we see in the plays of Euripides. This difference should not be seen as a shortcoming on the part of Sophocles, because his vision would not have been served by the kinds of characterization found in Euripides' plays. Nor was Sophocles unaware of these differences of characterization: supposedly, Sophocles himself said that he wrote men as they ought to be, while Euripides wrote them as they really are.

A long tradition of criticism holds Sophocles above both Aeschylus and Euripides, hailing his work as the apex of Greek tragedy. Aristotle praised him above all other playwrights, using *Oedipus the King* as a model in his highly influential *Poetics*. A very old paradigm treats Aeschylus' plays as the preparation for Sophocles' work, with Euripides' plays representing the decline of the art form. This model tends to draw heavily on the Aristotelian approach to dramatic criticism, but it says more about Aristotle's taste than it does about the three tragedians. More nuanced critical approaches make it almost meaningless to exalt one of the three men as "the Greatest." Although their lives overlapped and they lived in the same city-state, each man had his own unique voice and powerful vision. In the end, perhaps the frenzied descent into disorder so often imagined by Euripides was truest to Athens' fate: infighting and the dirty work of politics compromised Athens' good name, and Athens fell to her hated enemy, Sparta, just two years after the death of Sophocles.

Sophocles continued to write and serve in government well into his eighties. *Oedipus at Colonus* and *Philoctetes* are two of his last plays, and they are among the most praised works of classical art. He died in 406 BC. With only seven complete surviving plays, Sophocles left a legacy powerful enough to make him one of the founding fathers of Western drama.

About Antigone

The specific circumstances surrounding the origin of Greek drama were a puzzle even in the 4th century BC. Greek drama seems to have its roots in religious celebrations that incorporated song and dance. By the 6th century BC, Athenians had transformed a rural celebration of Dionysis into an urban festival with dancing choruses that competed for prizes. An anonymous poet came up with the idea of having the chorus interact with a masked actor. Later, Aeschylus transformed the art by using two masked actors, each playing different parts throughout the piece, essentially inventing Greek drama as we know it. With two actors and a chorus, complex plots and conflicts could be staged as never before, and the poets who competed in the festival were no longer writing elaborate hymns, but true plays. Athens was the only Greek city-state where this art form evolved; the comedies, tragedies, and dramas handed down to us from the period, although labeled generically as "Greek," are in fact all Athenian works.

After the defeat of the Persians in a decisive campaign (480-479 BC), Athens emerged as the superpower of the independent Greek city-states, and during this time the drama festival, or the Dionysia, became a spectacular event. The Dionysia lasted four to five days, and the city took the celebrations seriously. Prisoners were released on bail, and most public business was suspended. Roughly 10,000 free male citizens, along with their slaves and dependents, watched plays in an enormous outdoor theater that could seat 17,000 spectators. On each of three days, the Athenians were treated to three tragedies and a satyr play (a light comedy on a mythic theme) written by one of three pre-selected tragedians, as well as one comedy by a comedic playwright. The trilogies did not have to be extended dramas dealing with the same story, although often they were. At the end of the festival, the tragedians were awarded first, second, and third prize by the judges of Dionysis.

Although Antigone is grouped together with *Oedipus the King* and *Oedipus at Colonus* as a trilogy (sometimes called *The Theban Plays* or *The Oedipus Trilogy*), the three works were actually not written as a trilogy at all. It would therefore be totally erroneous to say that *Antigone* presents some kind of "final word" on the themes of the trilogy. In fact, although *Antigone* deals with the events that happen chronologically last in the myth, the play was produced in 441 BC - some 14 or 15 years before *Oedipus the King*, and a full 36 years before *Oedipus at Colonus*. Sophocles was clearly fascinated by the Oedipus myth, but inconsistencies in the events of the three plays seem to indicate that he wrote each play as a separate treatment of the story.

For modern readers, the Chorus may be the most alien element of the play. Greek drama was not meant to be what we would consider "naturalistic." It was a highly stylized art form: actors wore masks, and the performances incorporated song and dance. The Chorus delivers much of the exposition and expounds poetically on themes, but it is still meant to represent a group of characters. In the case of

Antigone, the Chorus is constituted by the Theban elders, old and powerful citizens of the city who watch and comment on the action. It interacts with the actors, and in *Antigone* the Chorus intercedes at a crucial point near the end of the play.

Consistent with the norms of Greek drama, *Antigone* is not divided into acts or scenes. The action flows uninterrupted from beginning to end. However, time elapses in non-naturalistic fashion: at certain points, from reports of what has happened offstage, it is clear that a great amount of time is meant to have passed even though only a few minutes have passed for the audience. In general, as noted by Aristotle, the action of most Greek tragedies is confined to a 24-hour period.

In his influential *Poetics*, Aristotle sets guidelines for the form of tragedy using *Oedipus the King* as his ideal model. Tragedy is usually concerned with a person of great stature, a king or nobleman, who falls because of hubris, or pride. There are unities of time, place, and, most importantly, action. Action may be thought of simply as motive or "movement of spirit": in *Oedipus the King* the action for most of the play is "find Laius' killer and stop the plague in Thebes." The action in *Antigone* is "preserve rightness and order in Thebes." *Antigone* is a strange case because the "movement-of-spirit" arguably comes from two directions: Antigone and Creon are both championing what is right, but they define rightness through different sets of values. Key elements include the moments of reversal and recognition, although not every tragedy has these moments. Reversal means a great and unexpected turn in events when the action veers around and becomes its opposite. Antigone experiences no reversal, but Creon does: at the Chorus' prodding, he finally backs down and listens to the advice he has been given, turning against the preservation of the kind of order he cherishes. Recognition means that a character gains sudden and transformative understanding of himself and the events he has experienced, moving from ignorance to knowledge. In *Antigone*, Creon finally recognizes that he has been misguided and that his actions have led to the death of his wife and son. Ideally, according to Aristotle, the reversal and the recognition hit at the same instant, as they do in *Oedipus the King*. While the *Poetics* are indispensable for the student of Greek drama - and, indeed, drama in general - Aristotle's theories should not be a straitjacket. Aristotle's guidelines make it difficult to appreciate the genius of Euripides, and by the standards of the *Poetics*, the great tragedies of Shakespeare would be failures. Aristotle is writing from a particular time and place, and he is also speaking from a very specific artistic sensibility. He may be the first word on Greek tragedy, but he is not the last.

In this ClassicNote, the quotations and the line numbers given with the citations match the lines in the David Grene translation; the reader is encouraged to look at different translations of *Antigone* to get a feel for the striking difference that a translator can make.

Character List

Antigone

Antigone is both the daughter and the sister of Oedipus (since he married his own mother). Now that Oedipus and his brothers are dead, Antigone and Ismene are the last of the Labdacus family. After her father went into exile, Antigone and her sister were raised in the house of Creon. Her brothers Polyneices and Eteocles were casualties in a brutal war for power, each brother dying by the other's hand. Creon has declared that Eteocles will be honored with burial since he was a defender of Thebes, while Polyneices' body is left to the vultures and dogs. It is this edict that drives Antigone to defy the state, since she believes her brother Polyneices deserves the same treatment as Eteocles. Some critics see Antigone as too self-righteous, even alienating, but others claim her as a seminal feminist, determined to do what is right even in defiance of patriarchal law. Indeed, Antigone captured the public imagination immediately after the first performance of the play more than 2,500 years ago, as her deeds expanded the possibilities of human action, reconceived the role of women in society, and delineated a new type of character, one who sets her individual conscience and belief in divine principle above and against the power and authority of the state.

Ismene

Antigone's last surviving sibling, Ismene is the foil for her stronger sister. In comparison to Antigone she has almost no agency, primarily because she is utterly terrified of disobeying men in power. She does not believe that women should ever violate the laws of men, since they are stronger and deserve subservience. Ismene does not help to bury Polyneices, but tries to claim responsibility for the burial later so that she can die with Antigone. Antigone refuses her help and Ismene is spared. This reflects both her great love for her family and her place as a symbol of the status quo who is rewarded for remembering her place.

Chorus of Theban Elders

The Chorus comments on the action and interacts with Creon, actively interceding with advice at a critical moment late in the play. The Chorus is comprised of the Theban elders, vital for maintaining order in the city, and Creon summons them to win their loyalty. They watch the unfolding events with sympathy and a discerning eye: they pity Creon and Antigone, but also comment critically on their faults.

Creon

The ruler of Thebes in the wake of war, Creon cherishes order and loyalty above all else. He cannot bear to be defied any more than he can bear to watch the laws of the state defied. He has Polyneices' body defiled while Eteocles is honored because he feels that he cannot give equal to share to both brothers when one was a traitor and the other was loyal. He does not recognize that other forms of justice exist, and in his pride he condemns Antigone, defies the gods, and brings ruin on himself.

Sentry/Watchman

The Sentry brings the news that Polyneices has been buried, and later captures Antigone. His speech is an interesting experiment in the history of Greek drama, as it attempts to approximate the rhythms and diction of natural speech. Similarly, his psychology reflects that of the simplest logic and reason - his only concern is preserving his life, and he asks basic questions, contrasting with Creon, Haemon, Ismene, and Antigone's lofty speeches on principles and ethics.

Haemon

Haemon is the son of Creon and Eurydice and is engaged to be married to Antigone. In a dramatic dialogue with his father, Haemon defends the moral basis of Antigone's actions while warning his father that the people of Thebes sympathize with her determination to bury Polyneices. He and his father part in anger, as he simply asks his father to do what's right for Thebes, and his father stubbornly follows the path of least resistance. Haemon's devotion to Antigone is clear; at her death, he is so distraught that he tries to kill his father and then kills himself.

Teiresias

Teiresias, or Tiresias, is a blind prophet who warns Creon that the gods do not approve of his treatment of Polyneices' body or the punishment of Antigone. Creon insults Teiresias, believing that he's simply blackmailing him for money, but the prophet responds with a prophecy foretelling the death of one of Creon's children and a warning that all of Greece will despise the king if he does not relent. Creon realizes that Teiresias has never been wrong and that he must do his bidding. The prophet is an important part of Sophocles' vision: through Teiresias, the will of the gods is made known, and his very existence implies that there is a definite will of the gods that is far above the domain of man's law.

A Messenger

The Messenger reports the suicides of Antigone and Haemon to the Chorus and Eurydice. He leaves to follow Eurydice when she runs off in grief.

Eurydice

Eurydice is Creon's wife and Haemon's mother. Broken by her son's suicide, she kills herself, calling curses down on Creon for having caused the tragedy.

Second Messenger

The Second Messenger reports Eurydice's suicide to the Chorus and Creon. Creon, already broken by Haemon's death, is forced to confront the suicide of his wife as well.

Major Themes

Pride

There is no question that pride, in the context of *Antigone* (and most of Sophocles' works), is a trait despised by the gods and punished without mercy. In *Antigone*, Sophocles describes the type of pride that allows men to create laws that substitute for divine principles. In other words, when Creon creates a law because he believes it is divine will, that is the ultimate display of punishable pride, for no man can ever create a law that is equal to or above divine right. As a result, when Tiresias comes with the news that Creon will suffer, Creon realizes that he has made a terrible mistake, and yet still refuses to admit it, bending to the prophet's message only because he wants to preserve his life, not because he knows he's gone too far. As a result, he must suffer the loss of his family.

Individual versus State; Conscience versus Law; Moral or Divine Law versus Human Law

These three conflicts are very closely related, but this crude set of pairings helps to untangle some of the central issues of the play. Antigone and her values line up with the first entity in each pair, while Creon and his values line up with the second. *Antigone* continues to be a subversive and powerful play, and the inspiration for generations of rebels and dissidents. In the 20th century, a version of *Antigone* rewritten during the Second World War became one of the most powerful texts of resistance against the Nazis. The conflict between the individual and the power of the state was as pressing for Greek audiences as it is to modern ones. Antigone is a threat to the status quo; she invokes divine law as defense of her actions, but implicit in her position is faith in the discerning power of her individual conscience. She sacrifices her life out of devotion to principles higher than human law. Creon makes a mistake in sentencing her-and his mistake is condemned, in turn, by the gods-but his position is an understandable one. In the wake of war, and with his reign so new, Creon has to establish his authority as supreme. On the other hand, Creon's need to defeat Antigone seems at times to be extremely personal. At stake is not only the order of the state, but his pride and sense of himself as a king and, more fundamentally, a man.

Gender: the Position of Women

Antigone's gender has profound effects on the meaning of her actions. Creon himself says that the need to defeat her is all the more pressing because she is a woman. The freedom of Greek women was extremely limited; the rules and strictures placed on them were great even for the ancient world. Antigone's rebellion is especially threatening because it upsets gender roles and hierarchy. By refusing to be passive, she overturns one of the fundamental rules of her culture. Ismene is Antigone's foil because she is completely cowed by the rule of men and believes that women should be subservient to them or risk incurring their wrath. Men are stronger, she says, and therefore must be obeyed. Ultimately, however, we see that she has merely bought into the problematic concepts that Creon espouses, for even when Creon realizes he may be wrong, he switches his defense, arguing that even if he were incorrect, he couldn't admit defeat to a woman, for that would upset divine law even more than backtracking on his principles. It is this fundamental untruth that Sophocles' play seeks to correct, mainly through the punishment that the Gods inflict on Creon as a result of his obtuse, misogynistic thinking.

Inaction/Lack of Agency versus Agency

When faced with injustice, Antigone and Ismene react quite differently - the former aggressively, progressively, and the latter more conservatively. Ismene is not so much afraid of injustice as she is frightened of her own demise - and she cannot bear to incur the wrath of men for fear of being condemned to the same fate as the rest of her family. After watching her father and brothers die, she believes that the best course of action is to lie low and obey. In the case of Ismene, it seems inaction is tied to fear-at least until she willingly offers to die next to Antigone, at which point we realize that she is not so much inactive as she is unsure of her place as a woman. Thus, while Ismene is a figure characterized principally by doubt, Antigone is one who plunges ahead purely on self-belief and her firm convictions about right and wrong. Ultimately, then, because of these fundamental differences in philosophy, they cannot die together, though Ismene wants to. Antigone forbids it - she cannot bear to have her sister tag along when Ismene all along is in the camp of the patriarchs, despite her eleventh-hour shift.

The Threat of Tyranny

Athenians, and particularly Thebans, were sensitive to the idea of tyranny and the fine line between a strong leader and a brutal tyrant. Creon is in many ways a sympathetic character, but he abuses his power subtly - mainly by decreeing man's law as a consequence of divine will. His faults do not necessarily stem from a lust for power, for he often has noble intentions. He is completely loyal to the state, but is subject to human weakness and poor judgment. Indeed, at the beginning of the play he frequently comments on his desire to do what's best for Thebes and gains the confidence of both Haemon and the Chorus of Elders, who say that they will follow him if that is his goal. And though he continues to reprise this theme, Creon is clearly more concerned with preserving certain values of law rather than the good of the city. When faced with a choice that would preserve 'tradition' or his own interpretation of the rule of law vs. a more progressive approach that does not follow precedent but clearly benefits Thebans, he chooses the former.

Short Summary

Polyneices and Eteocles, two brothers leading opposite sides in Thebes' civil war, have both been killed in battle. Creon, the new ruler of Thebes, has declared that Eteocles will be honored and Polyneices disgraced. The rebel brother's body will not be sanctified by holy rites, and will lay unburied to become the food of carrion animals. Antigone and Ismene are the sisters of the dead brothers, and they are now the last children of the ill-fated Oedipus. In the opening of the play, Antigone brings Ismene outside the city gates late at night for a secret meeting: Antigone wants to bury Polyneices' body, in defiance of Creon's edict. Ismene refuses to help her, fearing the death penalty, but she is unable to dissuade Antigone from going to do the deed by herself.

Creon enters, along with the Chorus of Theban Elders. He seeks their support in the days to come, and in particular wants them to back his edict regarding the disposal of Polyneices' body. The Chorus of Elders pledges their support. A Sentry enters, fearfully reporting that the body has been buried. A furious Creon orders the Sentry to find the culprit or face death himself. The Sentry leaves, but after a short absence he returns, bringing Antigone with him. Creon questions her, and she does not deny what she has done. She argues unflinchingly with Creon about the morality of the edict and the morality of her actions. Creon grows angrier, and, thinking Ismene must have helped her, summons the girl. Ismene tries to confess falsely to the crime, wishing to die alongside her sister, but Antigone will have none of it. Creon orders that the two women be temporarily locked up.

Haemon, Creon's son and Antigone's fiance, enters to pledge allegiance to his father. He initially seems willing to obey Creon, but when Haemon gently tries to persuade his father to spare Antigone, the discussion deteriorates and the two men are soon bitterly insulting each other. Haemon leaves, vowing never to see Creon again.

Creon decides to spare Ismene and to imprison Antigone in a cave. She is brought out of the house, and she bewails her fate and defends her actions one last time. She is taken away, with the Chorus expressing great sorrow for what is going to happen to her.

Teiresias, the blind prophet, enters. He warns Creon that the gods side with Antigone. Creon accuses Teiresias of being corrupt, and Teiresias responds that because of Creon's mistakes, he will lose one child for the crimes of leaving Polyneices unburied and putting Antigone into the earth. All of Greece will despise him, and the sacrificial offerings of Thebes will not be accepted by the gods. The Chorus, terrified, asks Creon to take their advice. He assents, and they tell him that he should bury Polyneices and free Antigone. Creon, shaken, agrees to do it. He leaves with a retinue of men to help him right his previous mistakes. The Chorus delivers a choral ode on/to the god Dionysis, and then a Messenger enters to tell them that Haemon has killed himself. Eurydice, Creon's wife and Haemon's mother, enters and asks the Messenger to tell her everything. The Messenger reports that Haemon and Antigone have both taken their own lives. Eurydice disappears into the palace.

Creon enters, carrying Haemon's body. He understands that his own actions have caused these events. A Second Messenger arrives to tell Creon and the Chorus that Eurydice has killed herself. With her last breath, she cursed her husband. Creon blames himself for everything that has happened, and, a broken man, he asks his servants to help him inside. The order he valued so much has been protected, and he is still the king, but he has acted against the gods and lost his child and his wife as a result. The Chorus closes by saying that although the gods punish the proud, punishment brings wisdom.

Summary and Analysis of Lines 001-241

Greek audiences may not have been familiar with the particulars of Antigone's story, but they would have recognized the setting of the play and the initial context of its plot - namely, the city of Thebes and the seeming curse that afflicts all members of the royal family. Before we begin to explore the details of this particular story, let's review everything that's happened before the beginning of the action.

Antigone is the son of Oedipus, Greek drama's most infamous figure. Oedipus was a king who married his own mother after killing his own father - not knowing that either were his parents. The story of *Oedipus The King*, Sophocles' most renowned work, is useful for giving us insight into Antigone's doomed lineage and should be understood prior to reading *Antigone*.

Oedipus is born of Laius and Jocasta, rulers of Thebes. Warned in a prophecy that Oedipus will grow up to murder his father and marry his mother, Laius and Jocasta arrange for his death - instructing a herdsman to kill the child. But the herdsman pities little Oedipus, and instead of killing him, passes him on to another herdsman from a neighboring kingdom, where Oedipus is raised by the king and queen as their own.

Later in his life, Oedipus himself hears the prophecy that he will kill his father and marry his mother. He flees the new kingdom, thinking he can avoid his fate. Along the way, however, he kills a stranger, who turns out to be his father Laius, and also solves the riddle of the Sphinx, saving Thebes and becoming her king (as well as Jocasta's new husband). The terms of the prophecy are thus fulfilled. Oedipus learns this only after he has been in power in Thebes for some time. A plague begins to kill the Theban citizens, and an oracle informs the king that Thebes is being punished because Laius' murderer dwells among them. Oedipus sets out to learn the culprit's identity, and soon discovers that Laius was the stranger he killed, and worse, that Jocasta and Laius were his true parents. Jocasta is able to put the pieces of the puzzle together some time before her husband-son, and in despair she hangs herself. Oedipus, upon discovering her body, blinds himself with her broaches and leaves the city, entrusting his daughters, Antigone and Ismene, to the care of Creon (Jocasta's brother).

In the days preceding the start of the action of *Antigone*, Thebes has been torn apart by war. When Oedipus fell from grace, his sons Polyneices and Eteocles were too young to ascend to rule, and so the kingdom was entrusted to Creon, the brother of Jocasta. The brothers soon reach the suitable age to take over, but they continue to entrust rule to Creon, knowing that a curse seems to follow their family. But soon enough, they begin fighting over who will rule Thebes - Polyneices, as the older brother, believes he has the birthright, but Eteocles ousts him, which sends Polyneices looking for refuge in Argos. There he raises a powerful army, which he uses to invade Thebes -- leading to his own death and that of Eteocles. Creon ascends to the throne once more. It is at this point that the play begins.

Antigone and Ismene meet at night in front of the city gates. Antigone has called her sister out for a secret meeting: she bewails their fate as daughters of a doomed mother and father and sisters of two men who have slain each other. She then informs Ismene that Creon has declared that Eteocles shall be given a full and honorable funeral, while the body of Polyneices will be left to the vultures. Anyone who tries to perform the proper funeral rites for Polyneices will be killed by public stoning.

Antigone asks Ismene to help her bury Polyneices, even though to do so would ensure both their deaths. Creon has "no right to keep me from my own" (I. 47). Ismene refuses because she says that they are women and must not fight with men - men are stronger and therefore must be obeyed. It is not her responsibility as a woman to "aim too high, too far" (I. 67). Antigone is furious with her sister and says she would no longer welcome her help even if Ismene granted it. She also says that she will die willingly for her brother and ensure he is given a proper burial.

Ismene cannot dissuade Antigone, and she leaves to perform the burial. Antigone encourages Ismene to proclaim her flouting of Creon's action to the world - she is not afraid of death, and believes she will die with nobility. Ismene is afraid for her sister, and cannot condone her actions...but she also understands that there is something to what Antigone wants to do: "Know this; that though you are wrong to go, your friends / are right to love you" (ll. 116-7).

The Chorus of Theban Elders celebrates the Theban victory over Polynecies, praising Zeus for destroying the arrogant Polyneices and ensuring that the "savage pair" dies so that the "sacred precincts" of Thebes can be free. Creon enters and addresses the Chorus, announcing that the city is safe once again. He tells the elders that they were loyal to Laius, loyal to Oedipus, and loyal to Oedipus' sons, and that he can only hope they will be loyal to him as well.

Creon says that a ruler must not be afraid to say what's right - no matter how unpopular his views may make him. He says he will never call a man a friend who is hostile to Thebes, and that the city is their lifeboat. Thebes has no friends, but he will make sure that the city is raised high. He further explains his edict that Polyneices is not to be buried or mourned, and rather left for the birds and dogs as a spectacle of shame. Creon orders the Chorus not to side with anyone who disobeys him. The Chorus believes that no one is foolish enough to ask for death, but Creon says that hope - and bribery - have often led men to destruction.

Analysis

In her very first speech, Antigone only briefly alludes to her and her sister's circumstances, but a Greek audience would have quickly filled in the gaps created by this 'in media res' device (meaning that Sophocles begins the story 'in the middle of things'). Antigone believes that they are the final victims of the curse that follows all the members of Oedipus' family. Oedipus, Jocasta, Laius, Polyneices and Eteocles have all paid their price - and now they suffer with shame and dishonor. Sophocles, then, sets up Antigone as an 'Oedipal' hero - meaning that she is structurally the protagonist, but cursed with a tragic fate. The question, of course, is whether we as readers can determine her tragic flaw - that element of her character that will send her to her doom - and whether we can successfully identify her antagonist.

Antigone is different from other Greek dramas in that it more a play of competing philosophies than a drama of 'action' or plot. Indeed, Antigone isn't allowed to just plunge headlong into her decision to bury Polyneices - instead, she must repeatedly explain herself in the face of philosophical objection. First in line is her sister Ismene, who argues that their family has suffered enough - their father died in hatred and disgrace after gouging out his eyes, their mother hanged herself, and their brothers killed each other - but now they're alone and must submit to the law. In Ismene's eyes, they are now women alone - and women must not fight with men, because men are stronger and control the law. Because Antigone refuses to kowtow to Ismene's reasoning, she has often been held up as literature's first feminist.

At the same time, there is the question of nature. Ismene, when pressed, argues that it is not in her nature to act - that she cannot possibly take up arms against the city. Antigone sees this as an excuse, but the converse can be argued - that it is in *her* nature to disobey, to bury her brother without confronting Creon first. Ultimately the sisters' argument comes down to a fundamental difference between the two: Ismene believes that her duty is to the men who make the law, while Antigone believes that "those who matter most" are the Gods, and that Zeus would want her to bury her brother.

The Chorus in Greek drama can serve a number of purposes, but here it is referenced specifically as the 'council of elders in Thebes,' meaning that it is a politically-minded group. They have lived through all the cursed relatives of Oedipus, and thus when battle against Polyneices ends, they see a time of rejoicing and the end of pain. The Chorus is not only civil, but also serves as the conscience of reason here. Indeed, when Creon appears, his first words praise them for having shown respect to all the members of Oedipus' family and to express his hope that they will accede to his rule (I. 165-170). In turn, he announces his latest edict, and the Chorus responds simply that they will do what he thinks is right.

As the play continues, however, we will note a growing involvement on the part of the Chorus as they begin to see that Creon is leading their city astray. For now, they are content to stay uninvolved because they believe that no one is foolish enough to risk death by burying Polyneices, suggesting that they assume the entire city is as tired of death, destruction, and misery as they are. It is too early to suggest that Creon is Antigone's direct opponent, but Sophocles has already hinted at Creon's tragic flaw. He believes in revenge - the idea that Polyneices must be 'shamed' in death in order to right his wrong - an act that seems directly antithetical to the

Chorus' wish to relegate the pain to the past (I. 206). Creon is thus perpetuating the legacy of Oedipus' curse, and we begin to see that as long as Polyneices remains unburied, the plague on Thebes will continue.

Summary and Analysis of Lines 242-525

The watchman arrives, clearly nervous about being the bearer of bad news to Creon. Indeed, he says that he almost didn't come for fear that Creon would project his anger about the news onto him - but then realized that if Creon heard the news from another man, he might be even more angry. Creon tells the watchman to spit it out, and the watchman says that Polyneices' body has been properly buried. The guards discovered the body - buried completely, with attention to ceremony, leaving no marks behind. There was no sign of wild animals, he says, and no dogs sniffing or tugging at the corpse. The guards began to blame each other before realizing that the only way to find the culprit would be to inform Creon. They held a lottery as to who would be the messenger of bad news, and the watchman lost.

The Chorus of Elders wonders aloud whether the gods are behind the burial. Creon is outraged, suggesting that the Elders are as stupid as they are old. He says that the gods would never have a caring thought for Polyneices - they know he is a traitor, and criminals are never honored by the gods. Creon says that money must be involved as a motivation for the burial and tells the watchman that unless he and his fellow sentries find the person who buried Polyneices, he will hang them all. The watchman insists that it is unjust to hold him responsible for the burial and soon leaves, declaring that he will flee, never to return.

The Chorus extols the nature of humans - their ability to master all beasts, to conquer land, sea, and air, to take advantage of language and mind, and to live in cities under law. The Chorus believes that man has the means to handle every need and never take steps towards the future without having the means to do so. The only thing man cannot master is Death.

The watchman enters, leading Antigone. The Chorus is aghast at the possibility that Antigone completed the burial of Polyneices, but the sentry confirms it. Creon returns, and the watchman informs him of Antigone's guilt. Creon demands details, and the watchman says that the guards uncovered the previously buried body and left it in the sun. Soon enough, they caught Antigone by her brother's side, renewing the burial. The guards caught her, and she didn't even put up a fight.

Creon asks Antigone if she did the deed, and Antigone says she will never deny her guilt. Creon dismisses the watchman and then asks Antigone, in a move that would likely spare her life, if she even knew that burying the body was forbidden. Antigone says that she did know, but she didn't believe it was a viable law. She says that she answers to Zeus, not to Creon. She further states that the gods didn't lay down these laws for human use and manipulation, and that she will endure the god's judgment of the burial, not Creon's, no matter now dire his punishment may be. Antigone adds that people who live in misery like her are better off dead.

The Chorus declares that Antigone is as unhinged as her father, but Creon says she is merely stubborn, arrogant, and boastful. If he does not punish her, then he is not a man - and indeed, Antigone would come across as the more "manly." He says that he doesn't care if Antigone is his sister's child - she and Ismene must pay for the burial. The Chorus is surprised that Creon would indict Ismene, but Creon says that they are both guilty, as they connived together over the act.

Analysis

The watchman is reminiscent of Polonius from *Hamlet* - namely, a character of slight absurdity who is there to provide comic relief amidst a dramatic expanse of tragedy. For all the philosophizing and melodrama associated with justice and idealism, here we have a sentry who is concerned with nothing else but preserving his life - even going so far as to continually interrupt Creon to ensure that he is going to escape unscathed and that things "won't be any worse than they have to be" (236). Though at times the watchman comes across as a bit buffoonish, he does serve a very clear purpose - to remind us that the danger facing Antigone is real, and that this is not a matter of simple bargaining over principles, but rather a dire battle over a person's right to live and die in accordance with divine or mundane law.

A number of scholars argue that Creon's tragic flaw is his obstinacy - his unwillingness to change his point of view once he sets upon it, but in this section we begin to see that his flaw runs deeper. He is afflicted with a sense of self-righteousness and the idea that man is meant to interpret the gods' will through law. In other words, he believes that human-imposed law is divine, and that a citizen who serves him is, in turn, serving the gods themselves. Upon hearing of the burial, the Chorus suggests that "the gods are behind this piece of work" (279), but Creon lashes out, demanding to know whether a criminal has ever been "honored by the gods" (287). There is, of course, circular logic in this argument, for who determines who is criminal? As the ruler of the kingdom, of course, Creon is the arbiter of who is criminal and who is not - and therefore reserves divine right for himself.

Creon reserves his deepest disdain for money, which he believes is the "nastiest weed to sprout in human soil." It seems a bit off-topic to go after money, even though he believes deeply that it is the source of bribery and therefore at the heart of the mystery of the burial, but Creon's diatribe about money gives us deeper insight into his tragic flaw. Indeed, money is ungovernable, for it falls outside the province of human law. In other words, Creon has full power over the lives of the citizens in his kingdom - the power to determine who is happy and who is not - but his power does not extend to the institution of money, which is beyond his control. Money allows for free will - and free will in turn, says Creon, ravages a city.

The Chorus' extolling of the human race is an extraordinary and quite famous passage in Greek drama. It is written as a Stasimon, and is known as the "Ode to Man." It is a fascinating piece of choral poetry that warrants analysis on its own terms - particularly its brand of implied philosophy about the evolution of man. Here Sophocles endorses a theory that says that man found his own means of survival apart from the gods - finding ways to tackle all sorts of beasts, weather, and terrain. This was a popular humanist theory of the time supported by several philosophers, but we're not quite sure of the Chorus' attitude towards it, because they seem possessed by both pride and fear. While man may have "taught himself" to handle every need through civilization, he has not conquered death - leaving him vulnerable to a mystery beyond himself. Furthermore, by allowing that man has found the means to survive and to transcend initial limitations, this theory also allows for man's potential downfall, since they are living entirely as a consequence of free will. As a result, man can "slither into wickedness" (367), or 'turn shameless' (372)...and can ultimately go wrong.

Antigone and Creon's debate has a number of fascinating implications. Antigone's argument is a rebuttal of the Chorus' "Ode to Man." She implies that man has no power over the rites to life and death - that these are functions of the gods, and that since Zeus made no announcement about the burial of Polyneices, she is free to bury him as she likes. The gods' laws live for all time, and no man can suddenly change them or manipulate the penalties surrounding them. Creon, meanwhile, sees such an attitude not as relating to the debate over the powers between man vs. god, but rather in terms of the mundane, mortal struggle between man and woman. For as long as Antigone claims to serve a higher power than Creon, according to Creon she "would be the man." Creon believes that Antigone must be killed to right the balance and ensure that no woman will ever best a man. Indeed, he believes that as long as he stamps out this woman who serves a higher power than himself, he will ensure that man's established laws always reign supreme. Ultimately, then, the battle between Creon and Antigone can be distilled to Creon's tragic flaw: his belief in the absolute supremacy of man's law. Ultimately, he will pay the price by seeing how little control he wields over both the will of the people and the will of the gods.

Summary and Analysis of Lines 579-785

Ismene enters, and Creon accuses her of being a conspirator in Polyneices' burial. Ismene confesses and says that she and Antigone were partners in the crime. Antigone, however, refuses Ismene's confession and says that she will not allow the penalty to fall on her sister. Indeed, she says she has witnesses from the gods of who did the work, and that she will not accept a friend who is only a friend in words. Ismene is devastated, and tells Antigone not to despise her. She says that they should die together so that they can sanctify their dead.

Ismene asks Creon whether he really would kill the bride of his son - since Creon's son Haemon is meant to marry Antigone. Creon says that there other women Haemon may find, and death will put a stop to the marriage. The guards take the two sisters inside. The Chorus mourns the tragedies of the house of Labdacus - the house that spawned Oedipus' doomed lineage. They say that madness stalks the family without fail, creating disaster for many generations like a great salt wave. They see grief falling from the beginning of the Labdacus history and that the gods continue to batter them without relief. Even the saving light of Antigone will now go out, doomed by foolish words and impulsive actions. They see madness as a product of mortals who are great, and all the members of the Labdacus family are subject to this curse.

Haemon enters, and at first seems willing to submit to his father's judgment. Creon embarks on a long diatribe, saying that a son must always be loyal to his father, disdain any wife who is hostile or criminal, look down upon all disobedience and treachery to law, and most of all ensure that they are not defeated by a woman. The Chorus is dazzled by Creon's speech, and now fully sympathize with him. Haemon, however, tells his father that the people of Thebes sympathize with Antigone - and that even though he agrees with his father, the will of the people should be honored. Haemon says that even though he would never question his father's leadership and agrees with the philosophy of his rule, he should also be open to other points of view. The Chorus also agrees with Haemon, and declares that both men have spoken well.

Creon is angry once again, and asks the Chorus whether they should be taught by a boy who is as young as Creon. Haemon tells his father he would never urge him to show respect for a criminal, prompting Creon to ask whether he thinks Antigone has committed a crime. Haemon says that he thinks not - because the people of Thebes deny it. Creon asks whether the people should tell him what orders to give, and Haemon says a place for one man alone is not a city. Creon accuses Haemon of being a woman's slave, to which his son simply replies that Antigone will not die while he is near, and that Creon will never see his face again. He exits, and the Chorus warns of the impulsiveness of youth.

Creon says that both girls will now be killed, but the Chorus' prudent questions make

Creon realize that Ismene should be spared. He does, however, say that Antigone will be buried alive underground with only as much food as religious law prescribes so that the city will not be cursed for homicide. Underground, Antigone can pray to Hades, since he is the only god that she respects. Maybe she'll arrange for him to save her life - and she'll learn that she's wasting her time showing respect for whatever lies in the underworld. Creon exits.

Analysis

It is interesting to note that Antigone does not defend Ismene out of love or altruism, but rather because she pridefully claims the burial as her own work. If Antigone has a tragic flaw, it's she - not Creon - who is too prideful, even boastful. When Ismene says that she'll be her shipmate in suffering (540), Antigone refuses her complicity, saying that the gods below saw who did the work, and more damningly, that "I won't accept a friend who's only friends in words" (543). Antigone, then, is saying that Ismene's sudden desire to claim responsibility for the act is not courage, but rather cowardice - for she'd rather talk than act, and would rather claim the spiritual reward than actually muddy her hands and do the right thing. Ismene, ever the pragmatist, asks Antigone why she's scolding her before Creon, since it "won't help her."

Creon, most tellingly, calls Antigone a "bad woman" when asked about his breakup of the Antigone-Haemon engagement. Indeed, he believes that when Antigone dies, there will be plenty of other women for Haemon to choose from, giving us an even deeper hook into his misogyny. Indeed, Creon has a precise conception of woman, and Antigone does not fit it. The impending marriage between her and Haemon is not a detraction from Antigone's execution, but rather an even more urgent demand for it. He cannot bear to have his son marry a woman who thinks she can ignore a man's laws. In fact, Creon would more likely want his son with someone like Ismene - who, we recall, told her sister earlier in the play that women must never flout the laws of men, and instead must obey them without the slightest ripple of rebellion. Slowly, we begin to see that Antigone is a play about women's roles in society - in other words, a pre-feminist drama.

Haemon enters with a very simple plea: "give me good advice and I will follow it" (636). He is not the typical headstrong, impulsive, hot-blooded Romeo that modern readers might expect in their romantic male lead - and indeed, though the Chorus continually ascribes him this characterization, we're not convinced by it. Instead, Haemon seems like the most practical character in the play - a man of intense reason, open to all sides, but requires that his father offer wise counsel. We sense that his tragic flaw is obeisance to his father at all costs. Creon, meanwhile, delivers a thunderous diatribe on what makes a man, but concludes simply that "order must be maintained" and there must be "no surrender to a woman" (678) for no other reason than that a woman cannot be said to best a man. He even goes so far as to imply that if a man had buried Polynecies, clemency might be in order.

Haemon, however, is concerned that the entire city is grieving over Antigone, and that no woman has ever had a fate that's so unjust. Haemon argues that his father need not believe that he is surrendering to a woman by allowing Antigone to live, or even compromising his beliefs - instead, he would simply be ensuring true, proper rule, for it is what the people want. Creon, however, is again fooled by his own preconceptions and ideology. It seems he has listened to Haemon, even possibly agrees with what he says, but he cannot bear to listen to or be taught by a boy like him. In other words, for Creon, circumstances do not matter, and context does not matter. He sees actions as absolutes - if a woman betrays a man's orders, she must die; if a young man tries to preach to an elder, they must not be listened to, etc. Haemon says that Creon should "look at what I do, not my age," but Creon again sees this as a matter of breaking ranks. Ultimately, there is no reasoning with Creon - he made his law, and it will be followed regardless of the costs.

Creon also possesses a mighty ego, in that he perceives everything through the prism of his own qualifications for rule. When Haemon suggests that Antigone's death will destroy someone else, Creon believes immediately that it's a direct threat from his son instead of thinking through the consequences of the girl's death. Indeed, it's obvious that Antigone's death will upset Thebes and devastate his son, but Creon is interested in neither consequence, concerned only with showing the people of Thebes who is in charge. Thus we see that Creon also believes that effective leadership involves follow-through at all costs, rather than reasoned interaction with his council, with his people, or with purported criminals. When Haemon points this out, Creon simply says that he's a slave - a woman's toy - prompting his son to wonder whether his father will ever listen. Creon's response is to threaten to kill Antigone in front of him, again confirming that for this king, it is action that makes a man, and not the ability to determine the consequences of those actions.

Summary and Analysis of Lines 786-1090

The Chorus extols the power of love, which affects all beings - including the gods. Love has the power to make even the strongest person go mad and pervert even the best minds - and the Chorus believes that the fight between Creon and his son can be traced to the wickedness of love. Aphrodite, the goddess of love, is undefeatable and makes all men toys in her hands. Love strikes the Chorus, too: they weep at the approach of Antigone, "making her way / to her bed."

Antigone enters, bemoaning her "last road" as she walks towards her death. Her husband is to be Acheron, "Lord of Death" (l. 810), and she will rest with him, deprived of marriage hymns. The Chorus tries to comfort her by telling her that she will be honored with hymns of praise, for she stayed true to her own laws. Antigone denies this, comparing her fate to the goddess Niobe who was locked away in "rocky growth" and was subdued into death. The Chorus sees this as a wonderful comparison - proof that Antigone is now immortal, like a goddess, but Antigone accuses them of mocking her and of trying to find a way to justify this cruel death where she has no place with human beings, living or dead, and no city to call home. Finally, the Chorus takes a stand and says that Antigone is extreme and impetuous, and deserves her fate because she went too far. She crossed the purveyor of high justice, and now must endure her father's legacy, which is eternal pain and punishment. Antigone weeps for her doomed ancestors.

Creon enters and says that Antigone should be taken away immediately - and left alone in her tomb. Antigone prepares herself for death, and says she is coming home forever now, to be held with her own people, most of whom are dead now under the curse of her family tree. She knows she has done the right thing, but still thinks that the punishment is too cruel. She's never had a man, never had a wedding, never shared love with a husband or raised a child. She will go to the hollow of the dead without ever knowing why - for she did not violate divine justice, and knows that the gods will not help her in her misery. She says that she doesn't know who to pray to, only that she does not want to repent for her supposed sin. She hopes that those who condemned her suffer as much as she does.

The Chorus sees her words as signs of her unchanged fiery character, while Creon grows impatient with the guards. Antigone tells the "princes of Thebes" to look at her, the last of her line, punished because she has given "reverence to what claims reverence" (ll. 1000-1). She is led away as the Chorus speaks of others who have suffered at the hands of the Fates.

The blind prophet Teiresias enters, led by a young boy. The old sage asks Creon to heed his advice as he has in the past. The signs say that the gods do not approve of the treatment of Polyneices' body. On the altars, there is "the carrion meat of birds and dogs, / torn from the flesh of Oedipus' poor son" (ll. 1074-5). The gods do not take the prayers or sacrifices of the Thebans, and the birds' cries are muffled because the birds' throats are glutted with the blood of Polyneices. Teiresias expounds on the importance of taking counsel, and says that a man who makes a mistake and then corrects it brings no shame on himself.

Creon accuses Teiresias of being a greedy manipulator. The ruler insinuates that the old sage has been bribed. Teiresias says that the wise should learn to heed advice, and he accuses princes of loving to take advantage of people. Then Teiresias gives him a prophecy: within a few days, one of his children will die because Creon kept one above the earth who should have been buried, while putting below the earth one who should walk among the living. The gods, as a result, will exchange a "life for a life." According to Teiresias, Creon has violated the proper treatment of both the living and the dead. All the cities will despise Creon, because the carrion animals will run amok, and birds shall carry the stench of death everywhere. The prophet leaves in anger.

Analysis

The Chorus functions not just as a literal set of characters - namely the tribe of elders - but also in a number of other capacities. First, they separate the key segments of action so that characters are given time to accomplish whatever they set out to do, and so that the audience can digest the heated emotions of the previous scene. Often, in thunderous dramas such as this, comic relief scenes and jester-like characters might serve the same purpose, but here the Chorus also offers tribute to the divine at every opportunity - to Zeus, to Love, to Bacchus, etc.

Of all the choral poems, the ode to Bacchus is perhaps the most unexpected, because love seems the one element most absent from Antigone. Indeed, for all his professed love of Antigone, Haemon seems genuinely unaffected by passion - making the Chorus' claim that the fight between Creon and Haemon is rooted in love rather unconvincing. Even more so, at the end of the play we're not sure whether it's love that causes Haemon's tragic end, or loathing for his father. It is fully appropriate, then, to wonder whether the Love the chorus is referencing is between Haemon and Antigone, or Haemon and Creon - for Haemon worships his father and only wants Creon to give him good advice for him to follow. Upon learning that his father is not only fallible, but mortally foolish, Haemon loses the one thing he held above all: his love for Creon.

Antigone is not an unfeeling heroine. Indeed, once she has been condemned to death, she doesn't doubt her decision, but rather continues to challenge the process of life that would allow foolish mortals to reign over divine law. These last speeches by Antigone are powerful and affecting because they seem to take her out of the bounds of the story - as if to literally ask, "why must I die when I've done nothing wrong?" For all her feminist claims, Antigone has no desire to be a martyr. We sense her desire to marry, to have a wedding, to have sex, to have a child - but now she has no one to pray to, because she has learned that the gods won't interfere on her behalf.

Her last speech is worthy of closer examination:

> City of my fathers, Thebes!
>
> Gods of my people!
>
> They take me against my will.
>
> Look, O you lords of Thebes:
>
> I am the last remnant of kings.
>
> Look what these wretched men do,
>
> For my pure reverence!

Antigone brings together all the horrors, dreams, and fears that have plagued her and will stay with her in her underground tomb. She appeals to the gods, imploring them to save her from men - for she is the last remnant of the true Thebes, the one that belonged to her father, and the one that belonged to the legacy touched by a divine plague. But now, for the sake of 'reverence,' or show to the gods, Antigone will die - and she asks that the gods intervene to show Creon that he is not acting in true reverence of the gods, but against them.

As in *Oedipus*, it is up to a blind prophet to make our king see straight, and Creon is aghast at Teiresias' terrible prophecies. Remember, Creon does not listen to Antigone because she is a woman, and will not listen to Haemon because he is young - and at first he won't listen to Teiresias because he thinks the soothsayer is only after money. Now we understand why Creon delivered the seemingly irrelevant diatribe on money earlier - because it gives him a convenient excuse not to listen to anyone who disagrees with him and isn't easily dismissed. Ultimately, however, he must listen to Teiresias, because the prophet is never wrong. In other words, Creon cannot argue with empirical evidence; he cannot argue with what he sees. Teiresias is himself offended, however, by Creon's initial dismissal of him and leaves with a precise understanding of Creon's tragic flaw - his projection of anger onto those weaker than him, his impulsivity, and his ego.

Summary and Analysis of Lines 1091-1350

The Chorus is terrified by Teiresias' prophecies, for they claim he has never been wrong before. Creon is shaken too, for the first time - and says he knows giving in would be terrible, but standing firm in the wake of such prognostication would invite disaster. He asks the Chorus for advice, and they tell him to let the girl go, and to build a tomb for Polyneices. They tell him that he must do it himself, as well. Creon takes his attendants and goes to follow their instructions. As they go, the Chorus sings the praises of Bacchus, and asks him to look over their city of Thebes and hear their hymns of praise. They need someone to assuage the plague over the Labdacus family and the Theban people, and they ask Bacchus to allow the people of the city to finally enjoy ecstasy. A Messenger arrives, revealing to the Chorus that great misfortune has befallen Creon. Haemon is dead by his own hand. Eurydice, wife of Creon, comes down to see the Messenger. She has heard that great horror has befallen her house, but she wants to hear the whole story from the Messenger.

Creon and his men gave Polyneices proper burial rites, as the Chorus had urged. After burying the body they went to free Antigone, but before going down into her tomb, they heard the sounds of Haemon, sobbing. Upon opening the tomb, they found that Antigone had hanged herself. Haemon was holding her body around the waist. Creon urged his son to come out of the cave, but Haemon instead looked at his father with poison and hatred and drew his sword against him. Failing to wound his father, Haemon turned the sword on himself.

When the Messenger completes his story, the Chorus notices that Eurydice is gone. The Messenger goes after her at the Chorus' urging to make sure nothing untoward has happened. Creon returns carrying Haemon's body, devastated by guilt, knowing that he has brought this plague upon his family. Immediately, a second Messenger emerges to inform Creon that Eurydice has killed herself. As she committed suicide, she cursed her husband. Weeping and bewailing his fate, Creon asks the servants to lead him away. No longer stubborn or proud, he knows that he has brought about the deaths of his wife and son. He stood by his conception of justice, but in doing so he defied the gods' laws and lost his son and wife. The Chorus comes forward to warn that pride brings retribution, and to declare that the greatest form of wisdom is an abdication of pride.

Analysis

Creon's most telling line in Antigone comes after Teiresias' exit, when he admits that it is so painful to "pull back" or give in to Antigone, since it "goes against my heart," but he cannot fight against "necessity," and thus goes to free her from the tomb. In other words, he still differentiates between what he believes is right and what must be done - in this gap, then, we see his tragic flaw. Indeed, if Creon suddenly threw himself on the mercy of the Gods, and begged forgiveness for the errors of his ways, the ending would be in doubt - for he would be redeemed in his judgment and the lesson would be learned. But instead he refuses all self-examination, and sees Teiresias' prophecy as something that simply must be "dealt with," as if it has nothing to do with the absolute truth. In fact, even when Teiresias is claiming the supremacy of divine law, Creon is still denying its power - implying that it's not right and doesn't deserve respect, but that still he will follow through with it because he doesn't want to die. Clearly, he will have to suffer in order to fully admit that he is incapable of seeing or setting the parameters for true law.

Haemon's death, according to the Messenger, occurred in a flash of rage - one that nearly consumed Creon as well. When Creon and his men opened Antigone's tomb, they found Haemon clutching the dead girl's waist. Haemon's first instinct was to stab his father - an expression of primal rage over both the murder of his lover and his father's fall from the pedestal upon which Haemon had placed him. Remember that upon Haemon's entrance all he asked was that his father guide him in the right direction, but now he sees that he's been led astray - and his first instinct is to destroy that which he once loved. But missing his father with his sword is symbolic of the larger problem - that Creon still has learned nothing, and that wounding him or killing him would simply give him more ammunition to support his disdain of the passion of women and of youth. In killing himself, Haemon sets himself free from the legacy of a cursed father and from a life without love.

Eurydice seems to play absolutely no role in the rest of the drama, but suddenly appears at the end to take her own life, merely adding to the body count. At first this may seem like overkill, but this moment is rather a precise fulfillment of the terms of Teiresias' prophecy. Indeed, Haemon's life is exchanged for Polyneices' - a death characterized by shame and vengefulness. Eurydice, meanwhile, will atone for Antigone's death - she dies much like Antigone, cursing Creon to the end, abdicating any sense of his self-ascribed power.

Creon asks for death, as his misery and guilt are too much to bear, but the gods do not oblige. Finally Creon is contrite - he knows that he killed Haemon and Antigone and shamed Polyneices, and that he can no longer be king or live among humans. In a final, cruelly ironic twist, he asks for the same fate as those he killed - a death of suffering - but the Chorus makes it clear that his destiny is to live out his days in the deepest regret and shame, as a symbol that no mortal can escape his divine fate. The Chorus ends with a distillation of the theme that it is wisdom - not power, money, love or good deeds - that is the key to a blessed life. With wisdom comes reverence from the gods, a disdain of arrogance, and the freedom from suffering that comes from believing in the omnipotence of man.

Ultimately, however, we're left with the question of whether Antigone is a true martyr - an innocent victim - or whether she also bears responsibility for her own death. Critics of the time made a number of charges against Antigone - all seemingly tied to her transgressions as a woman. She "leaves her home in the dark before dawn to conspire with her sister, and such activity in the dark is forbidden to women. She takes on burial, which is men's work. She does not accept male authority, and she threatens the order of the city by violating an order of the king" (Woodruff xvii). Perhaps most damning of all, she seems to make a conscious choice to give up the life of a woman (marriage, children, etc.) to stand by her principles - something that must have truly infuriated the men of the time. But Antigone's argument for the power of unwritten, divine law is particularly cogent and seems to deny any attempts to impose a tragic flaw upon her. Her reasoning, simply put, is that it doesn't matter what man conceives of as right and wrong for himself, and it certainly doesn't matter if these things are written in stone. Rather, it is more important to follow divine truth - the rights and wrongs of the heart - to ensure that man will live in accordance with the will of the gods. As a result, there is no precise law - only a guide what should be done in a given circumstance - and though she will be punished for her supposed transgression by losing her life, and regrets such a cruel fate, Antigone cannot take back what she has done because it is the only thing she could have done as a child of the gods.

Suggested Essay Questions

1. Why does Ismene object to Antigone's plan to bury Polyneices?

    Possible Answer:

    Ismene believes the men who rule Thebes must not be disobeyed because men are stronger and their will must be respected.

2. How does Antigone demonstrate pre-feminist ethics?

    Possible Answer:

    Antigone believes that a woman's duty is not to the men who rule a domain, but rather to her own instincts and her own sense of right and wrong. She believes that the gods do not dictate through a ruler, but rather through individual beliefs.

3. When does Creon become apologetic for his actions?

    Possible Answer:

    Creon never apologizes for his actions. Instead, he simply orders Antigone to be freed because he knows that Teiresias is never wrong - and therefore that his own life is at risk. However, he never truly believes that his order to imprison her was the wrong course of action.

4. What is the seeming reason for Haemon's suicide? Does he kill himself only out of desperate love for the dead Antigone?

    Possible Answer:

    Haemon's suicide seems to have two motivations - first out of anguish over Antigone's death, but also because he is so furious with his father for having betrayed his trust. Early in the play, Haemon tells his father that as long as he offers wisdom, Haemon will follow him. But now it is clear that his father led him astray, and for that Haemon believes that one of them must die.

5. Why isn't Creon killed by the plague that befalls him at the play's end?

    Possible Answer:

    Creon's punishment is to suffer without a family, and to suffer the guilt of knowing he destroyed the lives of innocents to preserve obsolete traditions and a misconceived legacy of misogynist rule.

6. What is Creon's tragic flaw?

    Possible Answer:

Creon's tragic flaw is that he believes that men have the right to interpret divine will and impose absolute power in their name. As a result, a simple belief - men cannot be wrong in the face of women - is elevated to law and thus leads to multiple (unnecessary) deaths.

7. Is Antigone ever apologetic for burying Polyneices?

Possible Answer:

Though Antigone bemoans her fate and believes death is a cruel and unnecessary punishment for burying Polyneices, she is never apologetic for actually covering his body. She believes until the end that she did the right thing.

8. Why does Antigone not allow Ismene to join her in her death sentence?

Possible Answer:

Antigone does not want her sister laying claim to an act that was solely hers for two reasons: one, because she wants her sister to remain alive, and two, because she wants her sister to feel the shame of abandoning her principles for the sake of staying alive and being subservient to men.

9. What is the role of the Chorus?

Possible Answer:

The Chorus is meant to reflect the conscience of Thebes - they are the elders who expect Creon to guide them towards wisdom. As they lead him astray, they begin to sense this and reflect their feelings in their choral poems.

10. What is unusual about the Watchman's speech?

Possible Answer:

Unlike the other characters, the Watchman's speech is written in more natural rhythms and dialect.

Antigone's Family Tree

An understanding of Antigone's lineage is crucial to decoding the significance of the various characters' ultimate fates. Let's examine the major characters in the family tree adjacent to this page.

Oedipus is a descendent of the Labdacus family, which is plagued with a terrible curse. Oedipus kills his father Laius inadvertently, not realizing who he is, and then proceeds to marry his mother, Jocasta, also not realizing her true identity. (For more on how this came to pass, see the summary of the first section of Antigone). As a result of Oedipus' marriage to Jocasta, he sires four children, who are at once his siblings and his children: Eteocles, Polyneices, Ismene, and Antigone.

Oedipus, shamed by his marriage and murder, surrenders the kingdom to his brother Creon (since Creon is Jocasta's brother, he is also Oedipus' brother). Creon takes over the kingdom because it is feared that Eteocles and Polyneices are also cursed by the Labdacus plague and will continue bringing misery to Thebes. Eventually, however, Polyneices makes a claim on the Theban crown, causing him to be banished. At this point, Polyneices raises an army, returns to claim Thebes, and ends up dying at the hands of Eteocles, who dies in the fray as well. Creon remains in control of Thebes.

Of this line, only Ismene and Antigone remain living at the start of the play. Antigone is supposed to marry her cousin Haemon, but by the end of the play, in a revelation that demonstrates just how widespread the Labdacus curse is - Haemon dies, Eurydice dies, and Antigone dies, leaving only Ismene and Creon as the de facto descendants of Labdacus.

Author of ClassicNote and Sources

Eddie Borey, author of ClassicNote. Completed on July 29, 2000, copyright held by GradeSaver.

Updated and revised Jordan Berkow July 31, 2007. Copyright held by GradeSaver.

Sophocles. Antigone. Chicago: University of Chicago Press, 1991.

Woodruff, Paul. Antigone. Cambridge: Hackett Publishing Company, 2001.

Kamerbeek, J.C.. The Plays of Sophocles: Commentaries III. Leiden: Brill, 1967.

"Novel Guide to Antigone." 2007-07-25.
<http://www.novelguide.com/antigone/index.html>.

"Antigone Bibliography." 2007-08-03.
<http://academics.vmi.edu/english/antigone.html>.

"Antigone: A Discussion of Her Biography and Nature." 2007-08-02.
<http://www.fjkluth.com/antigone.html>.

Essay: Influence of Antigone on A Doll's House

by Anonymous
October 14, 2001

It is very difficult to label something as a first in literature. Much the way inventions are often adaptations of previously patented objects, most authors borrow ideas and techniques form pre-existing media. In order to truly classify something as a first one must look for something entirely revolutionary, something that has never been done before. Two of these so called "firsts" include the first modern novel with Flaubert's **Madame Bovary** and what has been called the first modern play in Ibsen's **A Doll's House**. Regarding the latter, it is important to realize that while the play did break several molds which had endured for centuries, much was borrowed and adapted from past works. Of these, another "first" emerges for having shown a strong influence on Ibsen and his revolutionary play. Coincidentally, it is what historians refer to as on of the first plays in existence, Sophocles' Antigone.

In merely looking at the surface, one notices right away that both plays are significant in that they avoid the social temptation of using a man as a protagonist. Looking deeper into the stories, however, one can see that in even more contradiction with society, the female characters go against men. Both Antigone and Nora step into the spotlight as the female hero who has been put in a compromising situation and is forced to decide whether it is more important to follow what society dictates, or go with what they feel is moral and just.

Antigone is faced with the death of both brothers, one who is to be buried with full military rites, while the other, under dictate of the king, is to be cast aside and allowed to rot in the sun. She places family before the law, and ventures out to give her brother a proper burial. In A Doll's House, Nora too must decide where the line between right and wrong is drawn. In order to save her husband's life, Nora forges her father's name on a promissory note. Both women thus break the law using similar justifications. Antigone does so under the premise that the Gods dictated that all men deserved a proper burial. Likewise, Nora commits her crime with the belief that since it is saving a life, her situation is an exception to the rules.

The leading men in both works also have similar characterizations. Both Creon and Helmer are egotistical men, who put too much value on their position of authority; Creon so much so that he is willing to put a decree that defies the laws of the Gods. Furthermore, both are close-minded and too stubborn to see that they could be wrong. When Nora reveals her crime to Helmer, the audience expects to see a grateful and understanding husband, but instead is greeted with a spiteful and unappreciative man who does not see the true purpose of Nora's deed. Similarly, Creon, instead of seeing that his niece Antigone placed family and the Gods before the law of the land, solely sees that he has been disobeyed.

Both men worry about how their social status will be affected by the actions of the women; Creon is afraid he will look weak if he allows Antigone's deed to go unpunished, and Helmer is worried about allowing his wife to commit such a crime. One could argue that the true criminals are the men themselves, for not having the conscience to step down. Both men realize too late the consequences of their behavior. After yelling at Nora, and revealing to her in not so many words that she is merely a doll in his doll house, Helmer tries to apologize. Likewise, after much debate, Creon heads to the cave where he had exiled Antigone to free her. In both instances their apologies are too late. After Helmer's soliloquy, Nora walks out on her family to find a new life and discover herself. When Creon arrives to his destination, he finds Antigone hanged and his son dead by his own hand. It is due to both mens' stubbornness that their stories take this tragic turn.

While Sophocles and Ibsen are from two entirely different times and cultures, and although their writing styles differ dramatically, the influence of **Antigone** on the story of **A Doll's House** cannot be overlooked.

Essay: The Use of Light and Dark Images in Antigone

by Meredith Wilf
September 14, 1999

The "Golden Age" of Greece is notorious for its many contributions to the creative world, especially in its development of the play. These primitive performances strived to emphasize Greek morals, and were produced principally for this purpose. Antigone, by Sophocles, is typical. The moral focused on in Antigone is the conflict between physis (nature) and nomos (law), with physis ultimately presiding over nomos. Throughout Antigone, King Creon is a symbol for nomos, while Antigone stands on the side of physis. To portray these ideas, light and dark images are used as a recurring motif to reinforce the theme. Light is used to show something good that is happening, whereas dark is utilized to show show of something of which the gods disapprove. Following with tradition, this play uses light to portray what is right in the eyes of the chorus and darkness to reproach the other side. As the play is carried out, the chorus is constantly changing its opinions, first believing in the actions of Creon with respect to nomos, then unsure of what to believe, and finally seeing that Antigone's actions are more consistent with the morality of the gods and the truths of physis. Light and darkness are used to support in an emotional way the action of whoever the chorus is siding with at these various stages of the play.

It is clear that at the beginning of Antigone, the chorus favors the actions of Creon, or nomos. This is shown as Creon's intentions and retribution towards Polyneices are justified by jovial words and imagery involving light. In the battle between Eteocles and Polyneices, although both leaders were killed, Eteocles' army was the victor. To show that this was positive in the eyes of the gods, the first line of the Parodos in the Prologue refers to the battle as a "blade of sun". The morning following the battle was then called a "beautiful morning of victory". These are all positive feedback to the victory of Eteolces, and with the help of these light images, it is easy to identify the chorus' thoughts. Another praise to Creon is found in Ode I, where his law against burying Polyneices is referred to as "clear intelligence". In this instance, "clear" is used in the sense that it is easily visible, or obvious, making the statement positive for Creon. Later, in Ode I, the gods again side with Creon, as they refer to his decisions in lines 4 to 5, "Earth, holy and inexhaustible, is graven/With shining furrows where his plows have gone..." The gods are praising Creon; "shining furrows where his plows have gone" imply that he has left a good indent on matters that he has ruled on, in this case referring to the law against burying Polyneices. It is once again apparent that nomos is being favored by the chorus.

As the middle of Antigone approaches, the chorus seems to be unsure of whom to favor, and is torn between physis and nomos. Because of this, references to light and dark motifs in scenes two and three are ironic, and sometimes even contradictory. In lines 89 to 90 of Scene II, Creon claims, "...crimes kept in the dark/Cry for light". As

Creon says this in regards to Antigone, this statement, ironically, could apply to him as well, as his recent actions and abuse of his power could also be considered a crime. This comment actually foreshadows Creon's own fate. Another ironic instance is present in line 37 of Scene III, when Haimon says to Creon, "You make things clear for me, and I obey you." Clear is an ambiguous word, used here to show how Haimon is unsure of whose side to favor. Like the chorus, he starts out favoring Creon, but later sides with Antigone. Another example of irony comes when Antigone is doomed for death. As the time comes for her to get locked up and killed, she is feeling dejected and sad, and is looking for pity. Yet, she comes to realize that fate had brought her to this point, and it was not her fault, but was inherited by her from her father, Oedipus, and his family. Figuring this out, because Antigone has fulfilled her fate and realizes that she has not done anything wrong, she becomes spiritually immortal. She has succeeded in doing what she thought was right, (burying her brother), and she knows that the gods are on her side. This realization helps her to face her death. Yet, in line 7 of Scene IV, she continues speaking as if she has not figured this out. She says "...good-bye to the sun that shines no longer." This continues through line 50 of Scene IV where she declares, "...the very light of sun is cold to me." These statements imply that Antigone will die both physically and spiritually, although both she and the reader knows that this is not what will happen.

The final turn comes in the last two scenes of Antigone, when Creon finally realizes that he is in the wrong. He discovers that physis truly does supersede nomos, and, although he attempts to make amends, he is too late. Ode IV introduces this fact that the chorus has changed its mind, and Antigone's actions with the idea of physis are presiding over Creon's values with regards to nomos. It says, "Zeus in a rain of gold poured love upon [Antigone]." The word gold is a reference to light and contains positive connotations. This change in thought is ascertained in Scene V, when Teiresias tells Creon of his recent omen regarding Creon:

> I began the rites of burnt offering at the altar,
>
> But... instead of bright flame,
>
> ...the entrails dissolved in gray smoke,
>
> ...And no blaze!

Creon's omen states that the "bright flame", his previous time of being favored by the gods, also a light reference which hold positive connotations, has worn out. This is a symbol of Creon's pride, law, and power, which was abused , and has resulted in gray smoke, a gloomy image and a reference to dark. This shows that Creon's intentions are now not favored by the gods, as the gods saw that Creon's pride with connection to nomos was too high, and images referring to him are now dark and dismal. The play ends as the gods have turned their shoulder on Creon, and have made their final decision that Antigone is ultimately in the right.

Because the sole purpose of Antigone is to get a moral point across, the parallels between light and dark and physis and nomos are associated together, and used metaphorically to add diversity and imagery to an otherwise redundant script. In the first scenes, these light and dark images show the reign of Creon. These are followed by the indistinct and ironic middle scenes, and end with the gods choosing Antigone's actions over Creon's, leaving Creon spiritually dead and paying for his poor choices and conduct. These are very effective techniques, which allow Sophocles to more fully develop his play, and give it a more emotional edge.

Essay: The Use of Light and Dark Images in Antigone

Quiz 1

1. **Where and when did Sophocles live?**
   A. Sparta, 12th century BC
   B. Memphis, 8th century BC
   C. Syracuse, AD 3rd century
   D. Athens, 5th century BC

2. **The philosopher Aristotle wrote an influential text on drama called...**
   A. Four Dialogues on Drama
   B. Drama for Dummies
   C. Sophocles and the Art of Theatre
   D. The Poetics

3. **What did Greek actors wear?**
   A. Nothing at all
   B. Black and red garb
   C. Togas
   D. Masks

4. **Greek plays feature a group of performers who sing, dance, provide exposition and interact with the other characters. This group is called...**
   A. The Nymphs of Artemis
   B. Sappho's "maidens"
   C. The Chorus
   D. The Bacchae

5. **Who was Antigone's father?**
   A. Apollo
   B. Oedipus
   C. Zeus
   D. Creon

6. **Antigone's two brothers, Eteocles and Polyneices, did what?**
   A. Ate their mother's flesh
   B. Spied on Artemis while she was bathing
   C. Fought on opposite sides in a war for power in Thebes
   D. Were the greatest runner and discus thrower, respectively, at the
   Olympic games

7. **Who is Creon?**
   A. The new king of Thebes
   B. A failed applicant to the Academy at Lesbos
   C. The oldest man in Athens
   D. Antigone's fiance

8. **What happened to Eteocles and Polyneices?**
   A. They disappeared and were never seen again
   B. They were exiled
   C. They were chased by agents of the gods
   D. They died in battle

9. **What does the king of Thebes declare?**
   A. Antigone will reign in his place while he goes into exile
   B. Eteocles is to be given a funeral and full honors while Polyneices' body will be left for the sun and the carrion animals
   C. Thebes should have a drama festival to celebrate victory in war against the Persians
   D. Eteocles is to be left for the carrion animals and Polyneices thrown into the sea

10. **What does Antigone ask Ismene to help her do?**
   A. Bury Polyneices' body
   B. Start an armed revolt against Creon
   C. Accept their fate
   D. Escape Thebes

11. **What does Ismene do when Antigone asks her for help?**
   A. She refuses, and is unsuccessful in persuading Antigone not to do the deed
   B. She agrees to help her, but backs out at the last minute
   C. She refuses, and is successful in dissuading Antigone from the deed
   D. She agrees to help her, but is stopped by a sign from the oracle

12. **Who does the Chorus consist of?**
   A. The soldiers under Creon's command
   B. The Priests of Apollo
   C. The Theban elders
   D. The women of Corinth

13. **Which of these values does Creon praise in his initial speech to the Chorus?**
    A. Loyalty to the state
    B. Humility
    C. Moderation
    D. Compassion

14. **The Sentry character can be seen as an experiment. In the context of Greek drama, what is unusual about this character?**
    A. He wears a mask
    B. He speaks in verse instead of prose
    C. His speech is written in a somewhat naturalistic style
    D. He is a slave, but is depicted with great care and sympathy

15. **What does the Sentry report?**
    A. That Ismene has buried Polyneices
    B. That someone has buried Poylneices
    C. That someone is hiring mercenaries to fight Creon
    D. That Argos is preparing another attack

16. **The Chorus, on first hearing the Sentry's news, wonders if...**
    A. Oedipus' family will survive another war
    B. Antigone did it
    C. God did it
    D. Ismene might be trying to overthrow the government

17. **What does Creon tell the Sentry?**
    A. That he must find the culprit or he and the other guards will be demoted
    B. That he must pray at the altar of Zeus for forgiveness
    C. That he must leave Thebes in shame
    D. That he must find the culprit or face execution

18. **What/who does the Sentry bring back?**
    A. Guards, to fight Creon
    B. Antigone
    C. Polyneices' body
    D. Teiresias

19. **What does the Sentry witness?**
    A. A sudden and mysterious dust storm, which he takes as a sign of the gods' displeasure
    B. Antigone and Ismene fighting over the body
    C. Birds glutted with blood
    D. Zeus standing over Polyneices' body in triumph

20. **What does Antigone do when she is brought before Creon?**
    A. Defends her actions by asserting the supremacy of divine law
    B. Defends her actions by explicitly asserting that the conscience is the highest judge of morality
    C. Defends her actions by threatening to start an armed revolution
    D. Defends her actions by claiming that Creon has no legitimate claim to the throne

21. **According to an interpretation offered in this study guide, the motivations for Antigone's rush to martyrdom may have something to do with what?**
    A. The prophecies of Teiresias
    B. Creon's rape of Jocasta
    C. The social position of women
    D. Ismene's lust for power

22. **In comparing the two sisters, one could most convincingly argue what?**
    A. That Ismene and Antigone have never gotten along
    B. That Ismene is the brains behind the operation, and Antigone the muscle
    C. That Antigone consistently keeps her agency while Ismene seems to have very little agency
    D. That Ismene was their father's favorite

23. **What does Ismene do when she is brought before Creon?**
    A. She tries to rally the Chorus in support of the sisters
    B. She shrieks accusations at Antigone
    C. She tries to take some of the blame for burying Polyneices
    D. She tries to attack Creon

24. **What does Ismene argue about Antigone to try to convince Creon not to kill her?**
    A. That Antigone is princess and heir to the throne
    B. That Antigone is the most loved woman in Argos
    C. That Antigone is Haemon's betrothed, and thus Creon's future daughter-in-law
    D. That Antigone is a tireless champion of the city's poor

25. **Haemon, Creon's son, enters. What happens in their conversation?**

　　A. At first the two men disagree, but they finally come to terms with each other.

　　B. Creon orders Haemon to kill Antigone himself, but soon relents.

　　C. Haemon threatens to tell Eurydice what's going on.

　　D. At first Haemon seems to agree with his father, but when he tries to persuade Creon to spare Antigone the two men have a vicious argument.

Quiz 1 Answer Key

1. **(D)** Athens, 5th century BC
2. **(D)** The Poetics
3. **(D)** Masks
4. **(C)** The Chorus
5. **(B)** Oedipus
6. **(C)** Fought on opposite sides in a war for power in Thebes
7. **(A)** The new king of Thebes
8. **(D)** They died in battle
9. **(B)** Eteocles is to be given a funeral and full honors while Polyneices' body will be left for the sun and the carrion animals
10. **(A)** Bury Polyneices' body
11. **(A)** She refuses, and is unsuccessful in persuading Antigone not to do the deed
12. **(C)** The Theban elders
13. **(A)** Loyalty to the state
14. **(C)** His speech is written in a somewhat naturalistic style
15. **(B)** That someone has buried Poylneices
16. **(C)** God did it
17. **(D)** That he must find the culprit or face execution
18. **(B)** Antigone
19. **(A)** A sudden and mysterious dust storm, which he takes as a sign of the gods' displeasure
20. **(A)** Defends her actions by asserting the supremacy of divine law
21. **(C)** The social position of women
22. **(C)** That Antigone consistently keeps her agency while Ismene seems to have very little agency
23. **(C)** She tries to take some of the blame for burying Polyneices
24. **(C)** That Antigone is Haemon's betrothed, and thus Creon's future daughter-in-law
25. **(D)** At first Haemon seems to agree with his father, but when he tries to persuade Creon to spare Antigone the two men have a vicious argument.

Quiz 2

1. **What does Haemon warn Creon?**
   A. That Antigone is the rightful heir to the throne
   B. That Antigone is especially loved by the goddess Artemis
   C. That the people of Thebes secretly side with Antigone
   D. All of the above

2. **Early in their conversation, why does Creon insist that it is especially important that they beat Antigone?**
   A. Because she is a woman, and they cannot allow people to say that they were beaten by a woman
   B. Because she has supporters in the powerful city of Athens
   C. Because she insulted the god Dionysus
   D. Because she is the rightful heir to the throne

3. **What does Creon order in a rage?**
   A. That Antigone be stripped of her medals of valor
   B. That Haemon be executed along with Antigone
   C. That Ismene be exiled to Colchis
   D. That Antigone be brought forward to die while Haemon watches

4. **How does Haemon respond to Creon's order?**
   A. By running for his life
   B. By ordering the guards to seize Creon
   C. By refusing to watch and promising that he will never look at Creon again
   D. By praying to Hera for help

5. **Before the Chorus intercedes, what does Creon imply?**
   A. That Antigone will be burned alive
   B. That both Ismene and Antigone will be killed
   C. That both Ismene and Haemon will be punished
   D. That both Antigone and Haemon will be punished

6. **What does Creon decide after hearing the objections of the Chorus?**
   A. That Ismene and Antigone will be exiled to Colchis
   B. That Ismene will be hanged and Antigone will be sealed up in a cave
   C. That Ismene will be spared and Antigone will be sealed up in a cave
   D. That Oedipus' body will be disinterred and dishonored

7. **How could the Chorus' reaction to Antigone best be described?**
    A. As completely sympathetic towards her and her gender
    B. As angry
    C. As critical but sympathetic
    D. As a hateful condemnation of her and her gender

8. **Who is Teiresias?**
    A. A young prophet
    B. A deaf old prophet
    C. A general and former king
    D. A blind old prophet

9. **What does Teiresias warn?**
    A. That Oedipus' ghost is powerful still
    B. That the gods might destroy Thebes because of Antigone's defiance
    C. That the gods are displeased by Creon's actions
    D. That Antigone's rebel factions could destroy the city

10. **How does Creon respond to Teiresias?**
    A. By releasing Antigone and thanking the prophet
    B. By making offerings to the gods and thanking the prophet
    C. By rallying the mob to kill Teiresias
    D. By accusing Teiresias of corruption

11. **What else does Teiresias tell Creon?**
    A. That one of Creon's children will soon die and that all cities will hate Creon
    B. That three of Creon's children will soon die and that all of Greece will forget Creon
    C. That Creon will be forced into exile, but no city will take him in
    D. That Creon will die reviled

12. **After Teiresias leaves, what does the terrified Chorus advise Creon to do?**
    A. Give Polyneices his burial
    B. Give Polyneices his burial and release Antigone
    C. Execute Antigone
    D. Execute Teiresias

13. **What does the Messenger report?**
    A. Antigone murdered Haemon with a poisoned arrow
    B. Haemon was at the cave, and he tried to kill Creon before killing himself
    C. Both (a) and (b)
    D. After burying Polyneices, Creon and his men went to the cave and found that Antigone had hanged herself

14. **What does Eurydice do upon hearing what has happened?**
    A. She kills herself, cursing Creon before she dies
    B. She seizes the throne
    C. She tries on a poisoned dress
    D. She exiles herself

15. **What could this play be said to be about?**
    A. Conflict between divine law and human law
    B. Conflict between the conscience and the laws of man
    C. Conflict between the individual and the state
    D. All of the above

16. **Haemon's first instinct when his father uncovers Antigone's tomb is to kill whom?**
    A. The Messenger
    B. Himself
    C. Antigone
    D. His father

17. **The Watchman is concerned principally with preserving what?**
    A. His life
    B. Antigone's life
    C. The nation-state
    D. Ismene's life

18. **According to Creon, how many times has Teiresias been wrong?**
    A. None
    B. Eight times
    C. Twice
    D. Too many times to remember

19. **Who reminds Creon that Teiresias should be heeded?**
    A. Haemon
    B. Ismene
    C. Antigone
    D. The Chorus of Elders

20. **How do the guards catch Antigone in the midst of burial?**
    A. They get a photo
    B. She reenacts it for her sister
    C. They spy on the uncovered body
    D. She confesses to a crowd

21. **To whom does Creon say, "Where is your courage?"**
    A. Ismene
    B. Antigone
    C. Teiresias
    D. The Watchman

22. **Who tells Creon that as long as he gives good advice, he'll be followed?**
    A. Haemon
    B. Ismene
    C. Antigone
    D. The Watchman

23. **What does Creon believe is the nastiest weed ever to sprout in human soil?**
    A. Sex
    B. Pride
    C. Money
    D. Power

24. **Which god often serves as the reference point for all the others?**
    A. Aphrodite
    B. Mars
    C. Zeus
    D. Athena

25. **Who is the oft-mentioned god of the Underworld?**
    A. Haemon
    B. Zeus
    C. Hades
    D. Creon

Quiz 2 Answer Key

1. **(C)** That the people of Thebes secretly side with Antigone
2. **(A)** Because she is a woman, and they cannot allow people to say that they were beaten by a woman
3. **(D)** That Antigone be brought forward to die while Haemon watches
4. **(C)** By refusing to watch and promising that he will never look at Creon again
5. **(B)** That both Ismene and Antigone will be killed
6. **(C)** That Ismene will be spared and Antigone will be sealed up in a cave
7. **(C)** As critical but sympathetic
8. **(D)** A blind old prophet
9. **(C)** That the gods are displeased by Creon's actions
10. **(D)** By accusing Teiresias of corruption
11. **(A)** That one of Creon's children will soon die and that all cities will hate Creon
12. **(B)** Give Polyneices his burial and release Antigone
13. **(C)** Both (a) and (b)
14. **(A)** She kills herself, cursing Creon before she dies
15. **(D)** All of the above
16. **(D)** His father
17. **(A)** His life
18. **(A)** None
19. **(D)** The Chorus of Elders
20. **(C)** They spy on the uncovered body
21. **(D)** The Watchman
22. **(A)** Haemon
23. **(C)** Money
24. **(C)** Zeus
25. **(C)** Hades

Quiz 3

1. **Whose father locked her away from men because of an oracle warning against any son she might bear?**
   A. Antigone
   B. Persephone
   C. Danae
   D. Athena

2. **Who tried to suppress the worship of Dionysus, which led to his own madness?**
   A. Oedipus
   B. Lycurgus
   C. Polyneices
   D. Creon

3. **Oedipus married his mother, who was also his...**
   A. Friend
   B. Sister
   C. Aunt
   D. Niece

4. **Who did Oedipus inadvertently kill?**
   A. His father
   B. His mother
   C. His sister
   D. His brother

5. **Who is Creon the son of?**
   A. Thebes
   B. Oedipus
   C. Labdacus
   D. Menoeceus

6. **According to Haemon, Thebes sympathizes with whom?**
   A. Ismene
   B. Antigone
   C. Teiresias
   D. Creon

7. Who was a defender of Thebes?

A. Eteocles
B. Dionysus
C. Zeus
D. Polyneices

8. Who was cast out of Thebes?

A. Eteocles
B. Lycurgus
C. Polyneices
D. Hades

9. Teiresias is a prophet of which god?

A. Apollo
B. Aphrodite
C. Zeus
D. Athena

10. What is the name of Haemon's mother?

A. Ismene
B. Eurydice
C. Aphrodite
D. Narcissus

11. What is another word for "oracle"?

A. Chorus
B. Stasimon
C. Soothsayer
D. Antistrophe

12. How many deaths are linked to Creon by the end?

A. 2
B. 3
C. 4
D. 5

13. **How many times is Polyneices buried by Antigone?**
    A. 0
    B. 1
    C. 2
    D. 3

14. **Hades is the god of what?**
    A. Life
    B. Food
    C. Death
    D. Pride

15. **Who tells Creon that Ismene was not involved in the burial?**
    A. Haemon
    B. Ismene
    C. Antigone
    D. The Watchman

16. **What/who is Teiresias is led by?**
    A. A horse
    B. His twin
    C. A boy
    D. A goat

17. **How does Antigone die?**
    A. Hanging
    B. Burning
    C. Stabbing
    D. Beheading

18. **How does Creon die?**
    A. Burning
    B. Stabbing
    C. Drowning
    D. He doesn't die

19. **How does Haemon die?**
    A. Hanging
    B. Burning
    C. Stabbing
    D. Drowning

20. **Who delivers the last lines in the play?**
    A. Ismene
    B. Antigone
    C. The Chorus
    D. Creon

21. **The last words of the play extol the value of what?**
    A. Wealth
    B. Wisdom
    C. Pride
    D. Power

22. **Creon's last words involve him praying for what?**
    A. Wealth
    B. The return of his son
    C. The return of his wife
    D. Death

23. **The Chorus' poems are known as what?**
    A. Limericks
    B. Free verse
    C. Stasimons
    D. Apistrophe

24. **What is the name of Creon's son?**
    A. Agenon
    B. Jocasta
    C. Labdacus
    D. Megareus

25. How is Antigone related to Polyneices?

    A. She is his wife

    B. She is his niece

    C. She is his sister

    D. She is his mistress

Quiz 3 Answer Key

1. **(C)** Danae
2. **(B)** Lycurgus
3. **(B)** Sister
4. **(A)** His father
5. **(D)** Menoeceus
6. **(B)** Antigone
7. **(A)** Eteocles
8. **(C)** Polyneices
9. **(A)** Apollo
10. **(B)** Eurydice
11. **(C)** Soothsayer
12. **(C)** 4
13. **(C)** 2
14. **(C)** Death
15. **(C)** Antigone
16. **(C)** A boy
17. **(A)** Hanging
18. **(D)** He doesn't die
19. **(C)** Stabbing
20. **(C)** The Chorus
21. **(B)** Wisdom
22. **(D)** Death
23. **(C)** Stasimons
24. **(D)** Megareus
25. **(C)** She is his sister

Quiz 4

1. **How is Antigone related to Eteocles?**
   A. She is his wife
   B. She is his niece
   C. She is his sister
   D. She is his mistress

2. **Who says that they will have a "noble death"?**
   A. Haemon
   B. Ismene
   C. Antigone
   D. Creon

3. **Who/what does the Chorus praise at the beginning of the play?**
   A. The sun
   B. The gods
   C. The moon
   D. The stars

4. **Why is Antigone discovered burying Polyneices?**
   A. She returns to the site
   B. She leaves a pickaxe at the scene
   C. She leaves fingerprints
   D. She leaves her shoe

5. **Who wants to be Antigone's "shipmate in suffering"?**
   A. Haemon
   B. Ismene
   C. The Messenger
   D. Creon

6. **Why doesn't Creon listen to Teiresias at first?**
   A. Because he thinks the prophet is telling him the truth, and he doesn't want to hear it
   B. Because he thinks the old man is blackmailing him
   C. Because he thinks Teiresias is lying to him
   D. Because he believes Teiresias is an impostor

7. **Which family does the Chorus say has gone the way of madness and plague?**
    A. Labdacus
    B. Creonian
    C. Dionysian
    D. Hades

8. **Who took over the rule of Thebes after Oedipus fled?**
    A. Jocasta
    B. Eteocles
    C. Polyneices
    D. Creon

9. **Haemon says to his father that nothing matters more than Creon's what?**
    A. Search for a new queen
    B. Opinion of his marriage
    C. Determination to execute Ismene
    D. Advice

10. **What does the Chorus says that victory goes to in battle?**
    A. Madness
    B. Hate
    C. Love
    D. Pride

11. **According to the Chorus, which sin is punished most violently?**
    A. Envy
    B. Lust
    C. Greed
    D. Pride

12. **According to Creon, which is the only god that Antigone respects?**
    A. Lycurgus
    B. Aphrodite
    C. Zeus
    D. Hades

13. **Before she leaves for her tomb, who does Antigone say that she will be the bride of?**
   A. Haemon
   B. Acheron
   C. Cerberus
   D. Creon

14. **Who says "No city is home to me"?**
   A. Haemon
   B. Ismene
   C. Antigone
   D. Creon

15. **Antigone bemoans all of the following except...**
   A. Not getting to marry Haemon
   B. Not getting to have sex with Haemon
   C. Regret over burying Polyneices
   D. Not getting to have a child

16. **Who tells Creon that Thebes is siding with Antigone?**
   A. Haemon
   B. Ismene
   C. Dionysus
   D. The Chorus

17. **Who dies first?**
   A. Haemon
   B. Antigone
   C. Eurydice
   D. Creon

18. **Who dies last?**
   A. Haemon
   B. Antigone
   C. Eurydice
   D. Polyneices

19. Who finally confesses that Creon has seen where justice lies?

A. Haemon
B. The Messenger
C. Antigone
D. The Chorus

20. Antigone is sentenced to death by what?

A. Decapitation
B. Hanging
C. Burning
D. Burial live

21. Who calls Creon a childkiller before committing suicide?

A. Haemon
B. Ismene
C. Antigone
D. Eurydice

22. Who says that the men in charge must be obeyed?

A. Ismene
B. Antigone
C. Eurydice
D. Teiresias

23. Which city is also known as the City of the Seven Gates?

A. Thebes
B. Athens
C. Sparta
D. Hades

24. What is Teiresias' affliction?

A. He is deaf
B. He is mute
C. He is blind
D. He is missing a limb

25. **The chorus consists of...**
   A. 15 women
   B. 7 men and 8 women
   C. 8 women and 7 men
   D. 15 men

Quiz 4 Answer Key

1. **(C)** She is his sister
2. **(C)** Antigone
3. **(A)** The sun
4. **(A)** She returns to the site
5. **(B)** Ismene
6. **(B)** Because he thinks the old man is blackmailing him
7. **(A)** Labdacus
8. **(D)** Creon
9. **(D)** Advice
10. **(C)** Love
11. **(D)** Pride
12. **(D)** Hades
13. **(B)** Acheron
14. **(C)** Antigone
15. **(C)** Regret over burying Polyneices
16. **(A)** Haemon
17. **(B)** Antigone
18. **(C)** Eurydice
19. **(D)** The Chorus
20. **(D)** Burial live
21. **(D)** Eurydice
22. **(A)** Ismene
23. **(A)** Thebes
24. **(C)** He is blind
25. **(D)** 15 men

ClassicNotes

GradeSaver™

Getting you the grade since 1999™

Other ClassicNotes from GradeSaver™

1984
Absalom, Absalom
Adam Bede
The Adventures of Augie
   March
The Adventures of
   Huckleberry Finn
The Adventures of Tom
   Sawyer
The Aeneid
Agamemnon
The Age of Innocence
Alice in Wonderland
All My Sons
All Quiet on the Western
   Front
All the King's Men
All the Pretty Horses
The Ambassadors
American Beauty
Angela's Ashes
Animal Farm
Anna Karenina
Antigone
Antony and Cleopatra
Aristotle's Ethics
Aristotle's Poetics
Aristotle's Politics
As I Lay Dying
As You Like It
Astrophil and Stella
The Awakening
Babbitt
The Bacchae
Bartleby the Scrivener
The Bean Trees

The Bell Jar
Beloved
Benito Cereno
Beowulf
Bhagavad-Gita
Billy Budd
Black Boy
Bleak House
Bluest Eye
The Bonfire of the
   Vanities
Brave New World
Breakfast at Tiffany's
Call of the Wild
Candide
The Canterbury Tales
Cat's Cradle
Catch-22
The Catcher in the Rye
The Caucasian Chalk
   Circle
The Cherry Orchard
The Chosen
A Christmas Carol
Chronicle of a Death
   Foretold
Civil Disobedience
Civilization and Its
   Discontents
A Clockwork Orange
The Color of Water
The Color Purple
Comedy of Errors
Communist Manifesto
A Confederacy of
   Dunces

Confessions
Connecticut Yankee in
   King Arthur's Court
The Consolation of
   Philosophy
Coriolanus
The Count of Monte
   Cristo
Crime and Punishment
The Crucible
Cry, the Beloved
   Country
The Crying of Lot 49
Cymbeline
Daisy Miller
Death in Venice
Death of a Salesman
The Death of Ivan Ilych
Democracy in America
Devil in a Blue Dress
Dharma Bums
The Diary of Anne Frank
Disgrace
Divine Comedy-I:
   Inferno
A Doll's House
Don Quixote Book I
Don Quixote Book II
Dr. Faustus
Dr. Jekyll and Mr. Hyde
Dracula
Dubliners
East of Eden
Emma
Ender's Game
Endgame

For our full list of over 250 Study Guides, Quizzes,
Sample College Application Essays, Literature Essays and E-texts, visit:

www.gradesaver.com

ClassicNotes

GradeSaver™

Getting you the grade since 1999™

Other ClassicNotes from GradeSaver™

My Antonia
Native Son
Night
No Exit
Notes from Underground
O Pioneers
The Odyssey
Oedipus Rex / Oedipus
  the King
Of Mice and Men
The Old Man and the Sea
On Liberty
On the Road
One Day in the Life of
  Ivan Denisovich
One Flew Over the
  Cuckoo's Nest
One Hundred Years of
  Solitude
Oroonoko
Othello
Our Town
Pale Fire
Paradise Lost
A Passage to India
The Pearl
The Picture of Dorian
  Gray
Poems of W.B. Yeats:
  The Rose
Portrait of the Artist as a
  Young Man
Pride and Prejudice
Prometheus Bound
Pudd'nhead Wilson
Pygmalion

Rabbit, Run
A Raisin in the Sun
The Real Life of
  Sebastian Knight
Red Badge of Courage
The Republic
Richard II
Richard III
The Rime of the Ancient
  Mariner
Robinson Crusoe
Roll of Thunder, Hear
  My Cry
Romeo and Juliet
A Room of One's Own
A Room With a View
Rosencrantz and
  Guildenstern Are
  Dead
Salome
The Scarlet Letter
The Scarlet Pimpernel
Secret Sharer
Sense and Sensibility
A Separate Peace
Shakespeare's Sonnets
Siddhartha
Silas Marner
Sir Gawain and the
  Green Knight
Sister Carrie
Six Characters in Search
  of an Author
Slaughterhouse Five
Snow Falling on Cedars
The Social Contract

Something Wicked This
  Way Comes
Song of Roland
Sons and Lovers
The Sorrows of Young
  Werther
The Sound and the Fury
Spring Awakening
The Stranger
A Streetcar Named
  Desire
The Sun Also Rises
Tale of Two Cities
The Taming of the Shrew
The Tempest
Tender is the Night
Tess of the D'Urbervilles
Their Eyes Were
  Watching God
Things Fall Apart
The Threepenny Opera
The Time Machine
Titus Andronicus
To Build a Fire
To Kill a Mockingbird
To the Lighthouse
Treasure Island
Troilus and Cressida
Turn of the Screw
Twelfth Night
Ulysses
Uncle Tom's Cabin
Utopia
A Very Old Man With
  Enormous Wings
The Visit

For our full list of over 250 Study Guides, Quizzes,
Sample College Application Essays, Literature Essays and E-texts, visit:

www.gradesaver.com

ClassicNotes

GradeSaver™

Getting you the grade since 1999™

Other ClassicNotes from GradeSaver™

Volpone
Waiting for Godot
Waiting for Lefty
Walden
Washington Square
Where the Red Fern
   Grows
White Fang
White Noise
White Teeth
Who's Afraid of Virginia
   Woolf
Wide Sargasso Sea
Winesburg, Ohio
The Winter's Tale
Woyzeck
Wuthering Heights
The Yellow Wallpaper
Yonnondio: From the
   Thirties

For our full list of over 250 Study Guides, Quizzes,
Sample College Application Essays, Literature Essays and E-texts, visit:

www.gradesaver.com

13006629R00048

Printed in Great Britain
by Amazon.co.uk, Ltd.,
Marston Gate.